Small Habits

Simple, Tested and Proven Way To Break Bad Habits and Build New Ones

~ Richard Blake

Copyright Page:

Small Habits©Copyright <<2023>>Richard Blake. All rights reserved. No part of this publication may be reproduced, distributed or transmitted in any form or by any means, including photocopying, recording, or other electronic or mechanical methods, without the prior written permission of the publisher, except in the case of brief quotations embodied in critical reviews and certain other noncommercial uses permitted by copyright law.

Although the author and publisher have made every effort to ensure that the information in this book was correct at press time, the author and publisher do not assume and hereby disclaim any liability to any party for any loss, damage, or disruption caused by errors or omissions, whether such errors or omissions result from negligence, accident, or any other cause.

Adherence to all applicable laws and regulations, including international, federal, state and local governing professional licensing, business practices, advertising, and all other aspects of doing business in the US, Canada or any other jurisdiction is the sole responsibility of the reader and consumer.

Table of Contents

Chapter 1: "Bad" Habits vs. "Good" Habits.
- Using bad habits to achieve success.

Chapter 2: "It Takes 21 Days to Change a Habit".
- Changing Habits.
- What's so special about 21 days?
- Creating a fresh start.
- When habits are controlling and ruining your life.
- The will to choose.
- Goal setting.
- Accepting Responsibility.
- Searching for Answers.

Chapter 3: Negative Emotions and Positive Feelings.
- What is it you want?
- Creating Self-awareness.

- ☐ Keeping a Habit Diary.
- ☐ Root Causes of Bad Habits.
- ☐ Consequences.
- ☐ Making a commitment to yourself.
- ☐ Excuses and Inner Dialogue.

Chapter 4: How Good Habits Will Impact Your Life.
- ☐ The Benefits of Good Habit.
- ☐ Why Goals are essential for Happiness.
- ☐ Researching your Path.

Chapter 5: Stop Procrastinating and Get More Done.
- ☐ The consequences of Procrastination.
- ☐ Power Goals.
- ☐ Motivation and Enthusiasm.
- ☐ Interrupting Negative Behaviour.
- ☐ Keeping focused on the Benefits of Good Habits.

- ☐ Reward and Punishment.
- ☐ Eliminating Negativity.

Chapter 6: The Game Plan.
- ☐ Drawing up your Game plan.
- ☐ Power Goal.
- ☐ Asking for Help.
- ☐ Training wheels: Easing into New Habits.
- ☐ Timelines and Milestones.
- ☐ Dealing with Setbacks.
- ☐ Remaining Positive.

Chapter 7: Strategies for Successful Habit Formation.
- ☐ Using Reminders.
- ☐ The Power of Ritual.
- ☐ All Together now: Grouping actions.
- ☐ Keys to Consistency.
- ☐ Utilizing your Personal Rhythms.

Chapter 8: Living Positively.
- ☐ Thoughts, Belief structures and Habits.
- ☐ Affirmations and Declarations.
- ☐ Visualization and Positivity.
- ☐ Making a Vision Board.
- ☐ The Power of Hypnosis.
- ☐ Meditation And Clarity.

Chapter 9: Taking Action.
- ☐ Focus and Will Power.
- ☐ Implementation.
- ☐ Defeating Inertia.
- ☐ The Dangers of "All or Nothing"
- ☐ Accepting Incremental Improvements.
- ☐ Embracing Failure.
- ☐ Power of Persistence

Chapter 10: Keeping Score.
- ☐ A record of your success

- Weekly Progress Reviews.
- Celebrating Victories.
- Taking it To The Next Level.
- Breaking the Habit Permanently.

Introduction

When you think about it, much of life is something we do out of habit. From when we wake up in the morning to the actions we take during the day – our morning routine or usual breakfast, and daily work at the workplace are habits we develop to control 95% of our deeds. These unconscious thought patterns determine what we think, how we feel, and how we behave in almost any situation we find ourselves in. Because our habits determine all the little details that make up our daily lives, they are also directly related to the larger issues in our lives, such as how we earn money, how much money we get, the type of people we marry or live with, health and wellness and all other areas of our lives.

Our habits determine our character, the type of person we present to the rest of the world, and ultimately our fate. So, if we adopt bad habits – habits that negatively impact who we are – those very habits will prevent us from achieving excellence in life, and realizing our full potential.

Only by getting rid of bad habits and replacing them with good ones can we finally succeed in life and become the person we want to be. The purpose of this guide is to show you how to break bad habits - all kinds of bad habits, from those that are harmful to your health, like smoking or not wearing a seat belt, to those that can affect your self-esteem, like overthinking or overeating - and replace them with positive behaviors that can become part of your daily life and ultimately lead you to the results you truly desire.

Albert Einstein once said that the definition of insanity is doing the same task over and over and expecting a different result. When you keep repeating bad habits, it would be foolish to think that things will change for you. This book will show you how to stop the madness and start living life to the fullest by giving up bad habits and replacing them with positive ones.

Chapter 1: "Bad" Habits vs. "Good" Habits

When Is a Habit Really An Addiction? People addicted to drugs, alcohol, sex, gambling, or other self-destructive behaviors often point to physical and psychological addictions that prevent them from overcoming bad habits. But the truth is you don't have to be chemically or psychologically dependent to become addicted.

Addiction is defined as "the state of being enslaved by a habit or practice to the point that stopping the habit causes serious trauma". So basically any bad habit is an addiction because it enslaves us, preventing us from reaching our highest potential.

There will be consequences for reversing any bad habits. However, there is nothing to fear. The pain is temporary. Habits are not only helpful, but we rely on our habits to function in our daily lives. Physiologists tell us that out of the 11,000 signals we receive from our senses, our brains only consciously process about 40. So our brains memorize the words for us to focus on "higher-value" activities. Things like walking, chewing food, and talking don't require the mental focus needed to solve math problems or play video games. These activities we take for granted are habits we have developed that are done without intention.

Social habits work similarly. Most people shower at the same time every day or take the same route to work. These habits are carried out essentially without conscious thought. Bad habits like overeating, smoking, and speeding work in the same way. So how do you define a "bad" habit and what are the characteristics that distinguish it from a "good" one? In most cases the difference is obvious.

A habit is "bad" if:

1. It is disruptive, harmful, or poses a short-term or long-term danger to you or others.
2. It negatively affects your self-esteem, how others see you, and your overall reputation as a good or bad person.
3. It's a pattern of unwanted behavior that is acquired by frequent repetition.

Bad habits often start innocently. I smoked my first cigarette because my college roommate smoked and I was curious about what it was like. But bad habits tend to develop quickly.

A bad habit can act as a magnet for others. Smokers are more likely to drink alcohol. Drinkers sometimes use profanity or are rude to others. Rude people may hang around casinos or racetracks. Gamblers are more likely to associate with prostitutes or use drugs. Soon, what started as a strange or one-off event will turn into a self-destructive lifestyle that damages your reputation and can ultimately ruin your career, family life, and health, and even end your life.

Almost any habit that can be considered "good" can have a "bad" partner. Examples of bad habits are highlighted below :

1. Harmful personal habits such as smoking, drinking, and drug abuse.
2. Eating too much or not having a healthy lifestyle.

3. Making bad financial decisions
4. Gambling
5. Procrastinating
6. Addiction to sex or pornography

Anything that hinders your ability to live a happy and healthy life can be deemed a bad habit.

Using habits to achieve success
Often we are not even aware that we have bad habits. Have you ever known or worked with someone who had poor personal hygiene or had a friend who drank too much or partied too much? Usually, these people don't consciously decide to do their bad habits.

When we take the time to recognize our bad habits, take corrective action, and replace them with positive, healthy habits, the result is healthier and lasting change; health, prosperity, and happiness for our future.

Imagine you are a healthy, active person who exercises every day without thinking about it. Or someone who always makes the right food choices doesn't have financial difficulties, studies hard for every exam, automatically performs his professional duties perfectly, etc. Is that not desirable? If you could always make healthy, positive choices without thinking about it, your life would be a lot easier, wouldn't it? Once you can replace bad habits with good ones, you can also eliminate the stress and anxiety that those bad habits cause in your life so that you finally achieve the sense of happiness and well-being that you've always wanted.

Chapter 2: "It Takes 21 Days to Change a Habit"

You have embarked on a journey that will change the way you live. Once you accept the process of converting bad habits into good ones, the rewards you reap will be enormous and last a lifetime.

It doesn't matter how long you've had bad habits. It could be something you have done since childhood, such as lying or biting your nails. As long as you can recognize that habit is negative and you want to convert it into something positive, then you can turn any bad habit into a good habit.

Changing Habits

Everyone has bad habits. It doesn't matter whether it's the Pope or George Clooney, the Dalai Lama or the Archbishop of Canterbury, humans are human, they make mistakes sometimes and those mistakes can often turn into bad habits.

The problem is not that you have bad habits. It's normal. What is causing you unhappiness and emotional pain is that up until now you have not been ready to make a real commitment to change. You can do whatever you want. The human will is indomitable and the changes to come will surprise and amaze you.

What's So Special about 21 Days?
You may have been familiar with the notion that it takes 21 days to change a habit. This is one of the explanations why drug and alcohol rehab centers usually last 21 days. It takes the same time for the body to get rid of the toxic substances on which it depends. But it is also a time for the mind to expel the toxic negative thoughts that cause it to cling to bad habits and replace them with positive ones.

Three weeks or a month is also a good time frame to work on when changing habits because it fits into our calendar system. If you're targeting the first day of the month to start changing your habits, it's simple to use that month as a framework for working on your goal.

Not all bad habits take 21 days or a month to change. Some may take longer and some may take less time. For example, if your goal is to get up half an hour earlier each day to make your mornings more productive, you can make it a habit within a week to 10 days.

But habits that are ingrained in your personality — like being nicer to your spouse, becoming a more mentally focused person, or losing extra pounds making you fat and out of shape and replaced by muscle — can take months or even years to achieve.

Creating a Fresh Start

Everyone has experienced the frustration and helplessness that accompanies bad habits. When you do something that you know is harmful to you, but you still do it, it can cause emotional damage that can affect your self-esteem ("I must be a bad person because I always (Insert bad habit here").

But at the same time, bad habits can always be overcome as long as you persevere and apply the right strategies, which will be described in detail in this guide.

When Habits are Controlling and Ruining Your Life

Any bad habit can harm your physical and/or mental health, but some are more serious than others. While biting your nails may be unhygienic or especially healthy, it probably won't kill you like you would when you drink heroin or eat fast food every day.

Making bad choices almost always leads to worse choices. Even the most harmless bad decisions can sometimes lead to a downward spiral that leaves you wondering what just happened. Even the smallest bad habits can have a profoundly negative effect on the rest of your life. For example, tax fraud could result in "rounding up" on your hourly timesheets, which could result in "borrowing" your company's pocket money, which could lead to changing the books so that the additional money is transferred to your account. You have gone from a tax cheater to a fraudster.

The Will to Choose
However, you always have a choice. Even the most degenerate, emaciated, drug-addicted

street junkie or a 400-pound overweight person with diabetes, high blood pressure, and congestive heart failure can make life-changing decisions. This is one of the gifts to be a rational-thinking human being.

Thanks to the ability to reason, only humans can break bad habits and turn them into good ones. And it's never, never too late. All it takes is the will to choose and the courage to make positive changes in your life. This is the difficult part. As you will soon see, the rest is easy.

Goal Setting

Once you have passed the Rubicon and decided to make a positive change in your life, all you need to do is follow the process outlined in this guide and you can achieve your goal within the timeframe you choose.

Goal setting involves applying realistic expectations to desired outcomes. In Chapter 6, titled "The Game Plan," you will learn how to develop specific, realistic goals that you can take step-by-step to eventually lead to good habits and a happier and healthier life.

Accepting Responsibility

However, none of this happens in a vacuum. Any bad habits you harbor are yours and yours alone. Blaming others or circumstances for your bad habits will not help you overcome them.

Maybe your parents weren't responsible parents. Maybe your husband or wife is sexually indifferent to you. Maybe you were bullied at school. So what?

While these may have contributed to your bad habits, they won't help you overcome them. Any reluctance to take responsibility for your bad habits will eventually sabotage your efforts and prevent you from achieving your goals. Honesty and maturity are two key factors that distinguish between people who can successfully turn their lives around and those who are destined to repeat the same mistakes over and over again.

Searching for Answers

Just as you hold yourself accountable for your bad habits, in most cases you alone are not capable of completely overcoming your bad habits on your own. One way or another, you will eventually need help from others.

When we struggle with personal problems that are the result of bad habits, we tend to go around and try to protect ourselves. That's a bad idea. It's perhaps ironic that you're responsible for your bad habits, but you need the help of others - whether in the form of healthcare, nursing, coaching, support, or a prescription, simple information from books or websites - to improve things. But finding and getting the answers and help you need is an essential step in your healing process.

Over the next 21 days, you will experience many changes. Not everyone will fall into their "comfort zone". You may be used to being completely
self-sufficient and prefer to solve your problems completely independently of others but how's that worked for you?

Chapter 3: Negative Emotions and Positive Feelings

Many people are not even aware that they have bad habits. They just wonder why the universe keeps conspiring against them and granting them such terrible fortunes. They never even realize that in most cases they are the cause of all their problems because of the bad habits they keep repeating.

To make truly positive improvements in your life, the first step is to develop self-awareness. You cannot effectively choose new habits if you are not even aware of your current habits. In this section, we'll look at the process of becoming aware of your thoughts, feelings, and actions so you can see the connection between them and the things that happen to you in life. By developing this self-awareness, you can channel your subconscious thoughts and feelings into the realm of conscious thought, analyzing those thoughts so they can make connections between the bad habits and their impact on your life, then choose new behaviors based on what you learn about yourself.

What Is It You Want?

Everyone wants something out of life. For some, it can be a happy and fulfilling marriage. For others, it is unlimited wealth and power. For others, it could be spiritual enlightenment or a feeling of closeness to a higher power.

What do you want more than anything else in life? Try to think of the "big picture". Instead of just wanting to quit smoking, your goal might be to achieve optimal health. Instead of just paying off a huge debt, make your goal financial security or even prosperity for the rest of your life.

Creating Self Awareness

Once you've identified some overarching goals — think global, not local — the next step is to figure out what's holding you back from achieving those goals. This can be achieved by several methods, including:

Reflection: Think about past experiences, then use your understanding of how you behaved during those events so you can apply what you learned from them to future situations.

Friends and Family: Expand your relationships with others by asking people you trust if they see your bad habits.

Compare yourself to others: Think of people who already have the good habits you desire and consider what they do differently when faced with related situations.

Available Information: Are there any books, courses, or videos that can help you achieve your goals? What kind of things do you find when you search online?

Persona Beliefs: If you are spiritual or have religious beliefs, employ them to help you on your journey of self-discovery. Even non-religious people can benefit from submitting to the will of the universe, or a "higher power" if you want to call it that.

Start a Journal: It's nearly impossible to remember every thought and breakthrough you've had along the way. Keep a journal to track your progress and refer to what you've learned.

Create measurable goals: Start thinking about what success looks like. What measurable event must happen for you to believe that you have successfully achieved your goal?

There may be more than one bad habit that you want to change. If so, you may want to prioritize and address the issues one at a time. Trying to fix too many things at once can weaken your efforts thereby accomplishing little or nothing of substance. However, once you learn how to fix your first bad habit, the next bad habit will be easier to break.

Keeping A Habit Diary

Once you've chosen a single bad habit that you want to change, the next step is to develop an awareness of that habit as it applies to you. One way to do this is with a habit diary, which simply records your performance against your goals.

For example, if your goal is to quit smoking, you'll want to start tracking how many cigarettes you smoke each day and when you smoke them. If you want to stop overeating, write down everything you eat for the day. If your goal is to stop lying, then every time you lie to someone, write down what you said, who you told it to, and if you know why you said it.

This kind of tangible information will help you understand where you are relative to your bad habit. In many cases, the results you find and the patterns you notice can be shocking.

Root Causes of Bad Habits
After you identify a bad habit and start observing it in your daily life, it often leads to finding the root cause of your bad habit. While you don't want to blame others or circumstances for your bad habits — you own them, they're all yours — you can still try to figure out what's causing them.

For example, if your bad habit is using profanity too often, be careful when you find yourself swearing. Who are you? Which person do you never swear in their presence? Or if your bad habit is that you are addicted to gambling, what causes you to think about gambling? Do you have to go through casinos or racetracks on your way home from work every day? Is there a particular convenience store where you always buy lottery tickets?

Understanding the situations and motivations that cause us to act on bad habits will be very helpful later when we work on breaking them.

Consequences

The next step in developing your self-awareness of your bad habits is what I like to call "putting two and two together".

You thought about what you wanted in life before. You have identified the overall goals you want to work towards. Maybe you can already imagine an ideal life for yourself or have someone you admire living the kind of life you want. Now I want you to think about what is preventing you from achieving this ideal. What bad habits are preventing you from achieving your goals? In other words, I want you to "do the math" so you can see exactly how your actions are directly causing the effects you're experiencing. It is just cause and effect. Your bad habits are the cause. As a consequence, you're not living the life you want.

However, in your life thus far, you have not been able to put the two together and realize that your actions are having effects on you.

Making a Commitment to Yourself

So far, you have identified what you would like to change about yourself and have engaged in a process of self-awareness, understanding that the actions you take are responsible for the results you are experiencing.

All that remains is your personal and enduring commitment to change those actions so that you can change those consequences. All that is required is that you make a solemn and irrevocable commitment - a contract with yourself, if you will - that devotes you to achieving your goals.

It doesn't mean you have to change right here and now, and never pick up that bad habit again. Your life is too complicated for that to work. It probably took years, if not a lifetime, to get to where you are today. Promising yourself to change now is as effective as spitting into the wind.

Instead, take some time to think about what you're promising. Think about why being successful is important to you. How would your life change if you gave up bad habits? What would be the consequences of continuing to do bad things?

Excuses and Inner Dialogue

Once you've decided and committed to making positive changes in your life (which won't happen immediately or suddenly…it's a process), the next step is to stop making excuses or allowing negative inner dialogue to affect your decision-making.

You have realized that you are solely responsible for your behavior. It's not your environment, how you grew up, or how other people treat you. These are the kinds of excuses and negativity that people use as a crutch to justify their bad habits. Once you've committed to change, they no longer have any power over you.

Start paying attention to what you say to yourself right before and during a bad habit you want to break. What reasons do you automatically bring? What kind of reason do you use that allows you to do what you want to stop doing? These are the thoughts and feelings that you will have to overcome.

Chapter 4: How Good Habits Will Impact Your Life

Congratulation! The worst is over. Raising self-awareness to the point where you realize you need to change is the hardest part of self-improvement. Unlike 99.99% of people with bad habits, you can now admit you have a problem and take full responsibility for solving it.

The last chapter is the hardest part of the change process. Naturally, people do not want to admit their weaknesses or deny that they have a problem that needs to be fixed. However, this breakthrough is an essential part of the recovery process.

In this section, we will now focus on creating a positive environment that will give you the strength and support you need to cultivate a new habit for healthy life.

The Benefit of Good Habits
You may remember that about 95% of the things we do every day are due to habit. When you can get rid of bad habits and replace them

with good ones, positive things will automatically come to you.

Legendary inspirational speaker Earl Nightingale once said that if you're willing to spend an hour a day researching your field, you can achieve leadership in your chosen industry in just three years. One hour of study a day will make you a national authority in five years. And in seven years, you can become one of the most recognized professionals in the world.

Reading for one hour a day in your field equates to about one book per week. So you may find that something as simple as developing a positive habit like reading for an hour a day can not only bring positivity but can also change your life.

Just as a commercial airliner has all the important flight information programmed into the onboard computer so it can fly on autopilot, the good habits we develop are " mental software" that permits us to accomplish our utmost goals without having to think about it.

Step 1: Discovering Your Purpose
Developing self-awareness allows you to familiarize yourself with your current bad habits and connect them to consequences that are preventing you from reaching your ultimate goal.
The next step is to create goals for yourself to help you move away from bad habits and lead the life you want for yourself.

Goal setting is largely effective if you first have a positive vision and purpose for your life. This will get you inspired to work on "smaller" goals and habits that will help you achieve your overall goal.

This process can be represented by this diagram:

Purpose > Vision > Goals > Habits

The starting point is discovering your purpose. You can question yourself to do this:

- Who am I?

- Why am I here?

- What do I want to accomplish in my life?

- What will make me feel most satisfied?

- What do I value more than anything?

- How does this affect my choices?

Step 2: Creating Your Vision Statement
Think about the answers you find. Write them down somewhere and try to arrange them in some order or pattern. This is how you define your belief system, which is the main purpose of your life.

If you can't see the pattern right away, try thinking about these additional questions:

How would I choose to live if I could do anything in the world?
If you never had to worry about money again, how would you spend your days and nights?
At the end of your life, what would you name your most important achievement?

Are you starting to see it now? What you discover is your vision of how you want your life to be. The next step is to organize that vision into a sentence or a paragraph - known as a Vision Statement - that defines what you want out of life.

Step 3: Building Your Power Goals

Your vision statement is where you want to be. Your power goal is your plan for getting there. To develop these power goals, go back to the bad habits you've identified and want to break. Consider how this bad habit affects each area of your life:

- Health

- Relationships

- Money/Finances

- ☐ Work/Career

- ☐ Personal Development

- ☐ Friends/Social Life

- ☐ Family Life

- ☐ Spiritual

Not all bad habits affect every aspect of your life, but you might be surprised at how much harm bad habits can do.

To create a power goal, tie how breaking a bad habit improves each specific area you identify. For example, let's say the bad habit you want to break is gambling.

Your gambling addiction can make you lose sight of what's important in life, make you anti-social, financially unstable, and more likely to go into debt.

Power Goal: Breaking the bad habit of gambling makes life more positive, sets positive goals, and stops wasting money (the house always wins in the end).

Gambling has a huge impact on relationships and financial situations. When you're done breaking the habit of gambling, reconnect with your friends, family, and loved ones and work on improving your financial situation.

Continue this exercise with each category. If there is no direct connection between your bad habit and a particular area of your life, skip it and move on to the next step.

Why Goals are Essential for Happiness

Compiling a list of power goals provides a structure for building a game plan to achieve your vision statement. When that journey is broken down into small achievable steps, not only can you break bad habits, but you can essentially live your life on autopilot.

Long-term success is virtually guaranteed as long as you follow the plan consistently and habitually. Of course, things still don't work out, and life keeps throwing weird curveballs at you. But because you were able to quit your bad habits and replace them with good ones, you repeated the process over and over until all your bad habits were a thing of the past, which gives you the strength and personal determination to overcome any setbacks.

Researching Your Path

To achieve your Power goals, knowledge is important. The more information you have about your goals and how others have achieved them, the more tools you have at your disposal to reach them.

Spend some time on the Internet and research all things related to your goal. In particular, look for blogs and forums related to your biggest bad habits. Given the size and scope of the Internet, there are undoubtedly many Websites devoted to specific issues. You'll find a wealth of information and inspirational personal stories to keep you motivated.

Chapter 5: Stop Procrastinating and Get More Done

If the hardest thing about turning bad habits into good habits is admitting you have a problem, the second hardest thing is focusing on your goals. Life tends to get in the way of our intentions, and it's easy to get distracted or revert to bad behavior. It's also very easy to say in the abstract that you want to make positive change, but keep putting off the realization of that goal. This kind of procrastination can take months or years to reach your goals. It can even completely derail the weaning process.

The Consequences of Procrastination
Procrastination is just another excuse people use to avoid the hard work of reaching their goals. No one is responsible for your bad habits.
If you're hesitant ("I'll start next week" or "I'm not ready yet"), you're just cheating yourself.

You have every motivation in the world to change your life. But without direct and immediate action, you will never reach your overall goal.

Power Goals

Procrastination is often a problem. People think about the big problem instead of breaking it down into smaller, more manageable steps. It seems like the old saying: How do you eat an elephant? One bite at a time!

"Oh my god, I have to quit drinking", "I can't believe I have to pay off so many debts", or whatever your bad habits are, it can be discouraging. By breaking your goals into a series of easier steps and placing them in a series of well-timed events, you can make a positive difference without killing all your demons at once.

Motivation and Enthusiasm

Motivation helps keep you on your path to breaking that bad habit. This is either internal or external.

Internal motivation is what you do to help your decision to change your life. It could be reinforcing positive behavior with rewards or posting inspirational messages where you will see them often. Be creative. For example, if your goal is to lose weight, find the fattest photo of yourself, enlarge it, and tape it to the refrigerator door. This will make you think twice about sneaking into the kitchen for a late-night snack.

External motivation is when others encourage and support you to succeed. This could be a loved one or friend, a professional such as a therapist or life coach, or even someone who has written a book or made a video that inspires you.

The more internal and external motivations you use to stay on your chosen path, the more likely you are to be excited about the journey and to succeed and achieve your Power goals.

Interrupting Negative Behavior

There will inevitably be setbacks. No one is perfect. You may fail or give in to temptation. However, once you recognize the triggers associated with your bad habit, you can avoid this bad behavior by trying to stop the negative behavior.

As people develop the confidence that leads to recognizing their bad habits, they will likely identify many triggers and patterns that precede their response to bad habits. These can be thoughts you are having or physical sensations such as sights and smells that seduce you. Often, simply avoiding these types of triggers will get you back on track. But if you accidentally or unknowingly triggered one of these triggers, you can interrupt the potentially negative behavior by removing yourself from the situation and the thought processes that can get you into trouble.

For example, if your bad habit is alcoholism and you unexpectedly run into an old "drinking buddy", come up with an excuse to get away from that person as soon as possible. The more time you spend with this person, the more likely it is that you will trigger a craving for alcohol.

Keeping Focused on the Benefits of Good Habits

Temptation can be difficult to overcome. Especially early in the journey to breaking bad habits. One effective way is to remember why you want to break the habit in the first place.

Previously, we identified the benefits of replacing bad habits with good ones. These benefits are summarized in your personal vision statement. Keep these handy so you can refer to them again when needed. Keep a copy of your vision statement in your purse or handbag so that you can pull it out and read it if you find yourself wanting to go back to bad behavior.

Often, just remembering what you want in life and how avoiding temptation at the moment can help you reach your goals in the long run and empower you to make better decisions.

Reward and Punishment
Conditioning is a term used in psychology to describe the process by which rewards and punishments are used to influence behavior.

Experimental subjects can be taught learned behaviors by rewarding or punishing them when they fail to perform desired behaviors. Conditioning can also be applied in real life. You are rewarded with a salary, so you do your job. You pay taxes because you want to avoid the punishment of tax evasion in prison. As you break bad habits, using small rewards to reinforce positive behaviors can help you stay motivated and connect happy, healthy feelings to positive choices.

For example, if the goal is for you to lose 30 pounds in 6 months, build a reward structure that reinforces the achievement of various milestones.
Buy new clothes every time you lose 5 pounds or get a spa treatment along the way.

Punishment is not very effective, however, because people always find ways to "approve" unwanted behavior by abusing the structure of punishment. Usually not much is achieved with this model.

For example, if your bad habit is swearing and you have created a punishment structure where you have to pay $1 into your piggy bank for every swear word, you find yourself saving money so you can swear at your leisure. In other words, the punishment for bad behavior is "worth it". This is not a positive method.

Punishment also perpetuates negative thoughts in your bad habits. Punishing yourself negatively affects your self-esteem. So, to break bad habits, use lots of carrots, but avoid sticks.

Getting Rid Of Negativity

Removing as much negativity from your life as possible will increase your chances of achieving your Power goals. This includes both internal and external negativity.

Internal negativity includes critical, self-deprecating, and pessimistic thoughts and feelings about oneself. Notice when these types of thoughts and feelings arise and simply banish them from your mind. Through willpower, you can choose positive thoughts and stop negative thoughts.

External negativity can be hard to stop. These are things that other people say to you or express non-verbally that hurt your self-esteem. This includes hurtful comments from your boss, nagging from your wife, and "teasing" from your friends. If you want to increase your chances of hitting your Power goals, you should turn them off or lock them out.

Silencing them means standing up to those who criticize you and telling them that you don't care what they say, that what they say is hurtful and that you won't listen to them anymore. This is a bit more work, but it's an effective way to turn down naysayers while boosting your confidence. Still, it's not always practical. For example, if your boss criticizes your performance when you get your annual report, at least you want to keep working. In such cases, you can exclude them.

Just because someone has a negative opinion of you or says something mean or offensive to you doesn't mean you have to listen to them. Keep them out by not paying attention to what they say or by having them roll down like water off a duck's back.

Negativity must be banished from your life in whatever form it takes, as it is the enemy of your journey to achieving your vision statement.

Chapter 6: The Game Plan

You recognize your bad habits, make a personal commitment to replace them with good habits, develop a vision to get you where you want to be, and create Power goals to get you there.

The next step is to create a game plan that breaks down your journey into achievable steps. In my opinion, this is the most fun part of breaking bad habits and replacing them with good ones. Because you can build the structure you will use to bring your goals to life over the next few days or months.

Drawing Up Your Game Plan

Your game plan is a plan of action, such as that made by generals when leading armies and planning battles, or by industrial captains when planning expansion and increasing profits. It becomes a real, concrete plan with observable measurements, and built-in rewards designed to meet both short and long-term goals.

It starts with your Power goals. Pull these out and consider how long it'll take to get to them. Don't overindulge. Your game plan should challenge you to reach your goals as quickly as possible. The longer you stick to a bad habit, the harder it will be to stop it.

Let's see an example of what a game plan might look like. Suppose you gamble too much and want to stop the bad habit of currently going to the casino every Friday and Saturday night, buying lottery tickets every day, going to the racetrack every Sunday, and betting on sports several times a week. That's a lot of gambling!

When you identify my performance goals, the "family" goals you set were:

Family – I spend very little time with my spouse and children due to my gambling addiction. I also spend most of my income on gambling, which is often not enough to buy groceries or pay for their children's school fees.

Power Goals - Quit gambling so you can spend more time at home and support your family emotionally and financially.

In this case, terminating the cold turkey may not have a high success rate. You may have tried many times to quit, but you kept returning to your bad habits. Instead, Power goals can be broken down into a series of achievable steps with built-in reward structures.

1. At the end of the first week, I'll cut out the casino VIP club membership card, stop sports betting, and buy only one lottery ticket per week. On weekends, I'll use the money I saved to take my family out to restaurants.

2. At the end of the second week, I'll stop the Sunday "tradition" of going to the track and limit casino visits to one night per week. I will use the money I save to pay my children's school fees in arrears.

3. By the end of the third week, I'll voluntarily put myself on the casino's "banned guests" list and not buy lottery tickets. This will cure my gambling addiction.

As a reward, commit to planning at least one fun family activity every weekend, like going to the zoo or camping. Don't worry, there are no penalties for failure. If you fail to meet your one-week commitment, restart your watch and try again until you succeed. As long as you're engrossed and focused, you'll eventually work through your entire Game plan.

Asking for Help

Some bad habits are so powerful that it's almost impossible to break them yourself. Drugs, alcohol, gambling, sex, and other life-threatening habits may require professional help and the help and support of family and friends. Of course, you don't want to ask for help. People's pride and even shame often get in the way. But if your bad habit is so strong that you can't break it without help, you should put your reluctance aside and ask others for help.

There is no shame in wanting to be a better person. You may feel that admitting you have a problem makes other people think less of you, but the reality is that most people will praise you for trying to do something about it.

Training Wheels: Easing into New Habits
With very few exceptions, acting cool or trying to quit a bad habit right away is not effective. It will take a period at least. You can increase your chances of success by cultivating new good habits instead of trying to do it all at once. Break bad habits slowly (never too late) and establish new good habits to completely free yourself from bad habits and develop good habits.

For example, if one of your bad habits is drinking too much, you may want to cut down on your drinking and replace some of the time spent drinking at the bar with long walks or going to the gym. As the weeks go by, you can reduce your overall drinking and replace negative behaviors with positive behaviors. Over time, you will become "addicted" to exercise, proper nutrition, and a healthier lifestyle.

Timelines and Milestones

In most cases, it takes 21 days or a month to quit a bad habit. It's not required, but it's a good idea to start your game plan on the first day of the new month. This will make it easier for you to set the timelines and milestones you need to start building new positive behavioral patterns. If you can't wait for the start of a new month, at least wait until the start of a new week if possible.

When creating your game plan, don't just set goals for the first week and see what happens from there. To increase your chances of success, plan your entire game plan over several weeks until you reach your final Power goal.

When creating your game plan, the new week should build on the success of the previous week. This way, by the end of the process, you'll have eliminated the bad habits you were trying to break and replaced them with good ones which improve your quality of life and drives you to achieve your vision statement.

Dealing with Setbacks

Recognize in advance that you will experience setbacks. The trick is not to let a mistake derail the whole process. One of the benefits of the Game Plan is that if you don't hit your goals for a particular week, you don't have to start over.

Everything can be moved forward by one week and you can restart that particular week. Any other progress you have already made can be redeemed. If you experience setbacks, don't sugarcoat it, and go with your Game plan. It happened for a reason. Maybe you traveled too fast, or you didn't know how long it would take to reach a certain step in your journey. Go back and repeat the steps until you get it right. Only then should you proceed to the next step.

Remaining Positive

It's important not to fall into negative thinking just because you've failed. We are all human. Accept that anyone can make mistakes and move on. But don't dwell on the fact that you failed or think of yourself as a failure. The fact that you are trying to make your life better means that you are the opposite of failure.

It didn't always succeed, and even if it never succeeds, it can. Even Joe DiMaggio failed more than 60% of the time.

The most important thing is to stay positive and just keep trying. As long as you strive to be better, you are a winner.

Chapter 7: Strategies for Successful Habit Formation

Let's go back to defining habits for a moment. A habit is something you do without thinking, for better or worse. The familiar behavior happens automatically. It's a facet of who we are and how we live.

To develop a new good habit, you have to repeat it and train yourself until you do it reflexively without thinking about it. For example, if the bad habit you broke is speeding and the good habit you want to develop is sticking to the speed limit, you should force yourself to drive the speed limit every time you get behind the wheel and do it without thinking. Eventually, through repetition, it becomes second nature.

Using Reminders

Information overload is a very real condition in today's society and it is getting worse. Now that people can connect to the internet from their smartphones and tablets and stream videos anytime, anywhere, the result is shorter attention spans.

It's incredibly easy to get distracted now. Many other attractions will catch your eye. Achieving your Power goals and following your Game plan requires full and honest commitment. A helpful way to remind yourself to stay on track is with reminders. These are small things like sticky notes, text messages, emails, voicemails, etc. that you can send to yourself or have someone else send them to you to keep you motivated and focused on your goals.

Reminders are especially useful when used in conjunction with trigger points. If there are specific places or events that remind you of previous bad habits, use creative methods to post reminders for yourself to help you relapse. For example, if your bad habit is drinking too much and your trigger point is your family's liquor cabinet, padlock the cabinet and give your spouse the key so they can hide it.

The Power of Ritual

Doing the same thing at the same time every day can be a ritual experience. For example, let's say you have a "morning ritual" such as showering, drinking coffee, using the bathroom, getting dressed, and getting ready for work. They probably follow the exact same order every day, so you don't even have to think about it.

The same type of ritualized experience can be applied to newly developed good habits. Practice at the same time each day in the same order until the same movements come naturally. This way, you can take advantage of good habits without consciously choosing to do so.

All Together Now: Grouping Actions
When grouping actions, adopt a set of good habits and do them all at once. Save time, make it part of your routine and it will be done automatically.

For example, if the bad habit you want to quit is poor personal hygiene, then you can actually group good habits such as brushing your teeth, gargling, showering, shaving, applying deodorant, and wearing clean clothes and making it a constant ritual the same time each day. It is often much easier to act as a group than to try to remember to do each good habit individually.

Keys to Consistency

Something is a habit when you don't have to think on your part. Repeat daily for 21 or 30 days to ensure your new good habits are consistently implemented. If you keep doing the same thing at the same time, in the same place, and in the same order, you consistently follow new good habits as second nature. This allows you to create one good, lasting habit built into your daily routine, rather than multiple habits loosely tied together.

Utilizing Your Personal Rhythms

You may have already set up routines to follow at work, at home, and even socially. Instead of trying to install an entirely new routine, try to incorporate new habits into your existing one. This will make it easier for you to introduce new positive habits into your life and make them part of your ritual sooner.

For example, if disorganization is a bad habit, one of your Power goals might be setting aside time each day to organize what you want to accomplish that day. One established habit is to take a shower as soon as you wake up. By using your shower time to plan your day, you can adapt new habits to your existing ones. You can even set up a whiteboard in your shower to write down your highest goals for the day. Be as creative as possible!

Chapter 8: Living Positively

One thing many people are not ready for is success. Ironically, some people fail so many times that even when they finally break their bad habits, they just can't cope and fall back.

This is the kind of mentality that prevents them from accepting the fact that they are usually strong and strong-willed, and once they decide to do something they have the ability to do it to the fullest extent and see it through to the end. Clearing these types of mental blocks and harnessing the power of your mind to achieve and sustain success will help you achieve the long-term goals defined in your vision statement.

Sometimes your mind can limit what you can achieve. For example, let's say your bad habit is overeating and your Power goal is to lose 15 pounds within 30 days. If your mind has a defeatist or pessimistic attitude, it will be difficult to achieve your goals. In other words, the mind often guides the body.

Therefore, it is important to train your mind to reject the negative and accept the positive. It is possible to reprogram your mind to bring you more success. All you have to do is have beliefs that support your goals, and your reality will align with your beliefs.

Remember, habits work at a subconscious level and are based on what we believe or used to believe. But if you do not allow and suppress the persistence of negative thoughts, they will only persist until they are replaced by others.

Affirmations and Declarations

Pushing negativity out of our worldview is easier said than done. For most of your life, your negative thoughts have been reinforced by bad habits. In your head, you think you can't reach your Power goals because you've always failed in the past, right? There are techniques to expel negativity from your mind and replace it with positive thoughts. It is indicated by affirmations and declarations.

Affirmations are short phrases that you repeat several times a day, usually while looking at yourself in the mirror. They are designed to reprogram your mind to reinforce the positive and expel the negative.

Below are some affirmations:

"I am a powerful, willful person."
"I am strong enough to do whatever I truly want."
"I am a happy person who deserves success."

Affirmations can also be habit-centric:

"I am going to be sober today."
"I will spend my day smoke-free."
"I am going to stay out of the casino today."

By definition, an affirmation is a positive statement. Therefore, avoid affirmations using the words "won't" or "not".

Affirmations are a way to help keep your mind focused on something positive, and they do work.
Construct three or four affirmations related to your Power goals and in front of the mirror, repeat them out loud ten times a day for a week. By the end of this period, you will notice a shift in how you feel about yourself. You will have more positive energy and negative thoughts will be banished from your

worldview, at least as far as your bad habits are concerned.

A declaration is a statement you make to others about yourself. Like affirmations, they work by defining who you are to yourself and others.

For example, someone who attends an Alcoholics Anonymous meeting always commences "sharing" by saying, "My name is (whatever your name is) and I am an alcoholic." By declaring, the person takes responsibility publicly that he or she has a problem, while at the same time receiving support from the group.

Affirmations and declarations are effective ways to build positive feelings and drive negative thoughts out of your mind. It may feel a little silly at first, but once you realize the benefits, that embarrassment quickly turns into a feeling of empowerment.

Visualization and Positivity

Another way to encourage positivity is through visualization exercises. This is when you take a moment each day to imagine what your life would be like if you replaced your bad habits with good ones.

Find a quiet place where you won't be disturbed for at least 5-10 minutes and try it yourself. Sit comfortably and close your eyes. Try to relax completely. When your mind is quiet, instead of dwelling on bad habits and their consequences, imagine what your daily life would look like if you developed new good habits.

Please be as detailed as possible. What will other people say to you? What do you feel? What are your thoughts? What will you look like?

Visualization helps prepare you for success by foreseeing success. Second, when you start to see the positive consequences of your good habits, you are less likely to reject them with pessimism. I believe that by visualizing events, we can influence them positively. So, just because you believe positive things will happen to you, positive things can actually happen.

There may or may not be a direct correlation between the two, but preparing your mind for success through visualization can make it easier to accept it when it comes.

Making a Vision Board

Different people learn in different ways. Some people are doers and need to get their hands dirty by actually completing certain tasks. Others can learn how to do something by reading a book or watching a video. Others, however, are visual learners who need to physically see something repeatedly before they can absorb it into their minds. That's what vision boards are for. A vision board is a collection of photos, images, quotes, videos, and other things that positively reinforce what you're trying to achieve. This can be a collage of cardboard or magazine clippings, or a digital web page created on Pinterest or another website.

Either way, the purpose of a vision board is to visually reinforce your goals. By glancing at your vision board often, you can train your mind to think positively about your journey. This will ease the process of making positive decisions and avoiding negative ones.

The Power of Hypnosis

Hypnosis has a bad reputation with some people because of scammers and fakeparty entertainers, but hypnosis is widely used in psychology and psychiatry to treat various mental illnesses. It is an actual physiological process.

When hypnotized by a trained professional, the subject is put into a deeply relaxed trance-like state, and post-hypnotic suggestions work on the person's subconscious mind. These suggestions are then incorporated into their belief system, but only if they are disposed to them first.

For example, you can't hypnotize someone into believing in God if they're already an agnostic or an Atheist, or vote Democrat if they're a Republican. For this reason, people who are struggling to quit may be hypnotized into believing that their cigarettes taste like poison. When a person comes out of hypnosis, this suggestion remains part of their belief system, and they can smoke because they are afraid of the bad taste of smoking.

If you are interested in using hypnosis to break bad habits, ask your doctor or health care professional for a referral to a reputable professional hypnotist. There are also inexpensive shortcuts you can find online that use self-hypnosis programs developed by experts. Self-hypnosis tapes and CDs purchased online can help you relax and address underlying issues and thereby helping you break bad habits.

Meditation and Clarity

When you do the visualization exercise, you are already doing some form of meditation. Meditation works in the same way.
Find a quiet spot where you won't be disturbed and settle into the relaxing atmosphere. The difference is that when you meditate, instead of visualizing yourself as successful, you completely clear all your thoughts.

When in a meditative state your mind is a blank page. No distractions or fears occupy your mind for a period of time (usually 10-30 minutes), clear your mind of everything. After coming out of the meditative state, you will feel relaxed and completely rejuvenated. Just 15-20 minutes of meditation can give you as much energy as a full night's sleep. Fear is reduced and negative thoughts are suppressed. It also makes your mind sharper and clearer, helping you to think more clearly and allowing you to achieve your Power goals more easily.

Chapter 9: Taking Action

The Chinese philosopher Confucius famously said, "A journey of a thousand miles starts with a single step" more than 2,500 years ago, and it is as true today as it was the day it was said.

Now that you have a game plan complete with timetables, milestones, measurable goals, and rewards, the next step is to implement it. Making big changes in life can be scary for some and others become anxious. But you should be neither scared nor anxious seeing you want to make a sincere change in the way your life is headed.

Focus and Willpower

The time and energy you put into creating your game plan will pay off when you start your journey. Knowing in advance where you need to be at every step helps you stay focused and motivated.

Still, unpredictable surprises always happen, and life throws curveballs at you from time to time. The fundamental changes you are making now will have a positive impact on all aspects of your life going forward.

If you start to get stuck, use the techniques outlined in the previous chapter (affirmations, vision boards, meditation, etc.) to keep you on track.

Implementation

Waking up on the first day of the program, changing bad habits, and replacing them with good ones can make you feel nervous and anxious. Calm down to the fact that you have planned every step of the way. You already have all the tools you need to break bad habits.

The road is long, but the steps are short. I can do it! Not only is success inevitable, but given your drive and the structure you've put in place to prepare for the journey, you're completely prepared. You are strong, brave, and capable. Everything before now has been a prologue. Now is the moment when real, genuine, positive change begins. Are you excited? you have to!

Defeating Inertia

Newton's first law of motion states that objects in motion tend to stay in motion, and objects at rest tend to stay at rest. This law can readily be used for habits. It's much easier to stay where you are than to change.

But without change, there is no growth. And without growth, you cannot achieve the success you desire. Luckily, you don't have to use overwhelming force to get the ball rolling. A slight tweak in the right direction and you're on your way. As you progress through your game plan and hit your goals, the momentum builds and before you know it you're halfway through your goal, past the 3rd or 4th quarters, and finally in sight of the line.

The Dangers of "All or Nothing"
Something is better than nothing. The end goal can be pretty daunting, but expecting to jump from point A to the finish line in one step is usually unrealistic. It doesn't work that way. Try as much as you can to avoid this approach. It's nothing but frustration. Most of the time, bad habits can be broken with smaller,

achievable steps backed by internal and external positivity and ongoing motivation.

Accepting Incremental Improvements
You don't have to eat the enchiladas all at once. It's better to take a few bites than to choke or overload your digestive tract. Your bad habits didn't pick up overnight, so you shouldn't expect to be able to fix them almost immediately.

For example, if your bad habit is taking up heroin, going cold turkey can be an intolerable adventure. It can shock your system and make the cure worse than the disease. Depending on your level of addiction- it may cause death. A better plan is to slowly wean yourself off the drug under the care of a trusted doctor. They may propose that you replace heroin with a less harmful drug so that the procedure of eradicating your addiction becomes more attainable.

The same principles apply even if your bad habits are less radical. Embrace incremental improvements. Ultimately, they lead to breaking your bad habits once and for all.

Embracing Failure

For those with a negative outlook, failure is terrifying and should be avoided at all costs. But for those with a positive mindset, failure is an opportunity.

As humans, we learn from our mistakes. It's the "error" of the trial and error part that leads to the biggest discoveries. If you get frustrated along the way or miss your Game Plan weekly goals, use this as a learning tool to understand what went wrong and why. That way, you get to avoid similar mistakes subsequently. The beauty of habit-breaking programs is that if you fail, you don't have to start over. All you have to do is maintain momentum by simply repeating the steps you slipped down.

Power of Persistence

By harnessing the power of Persistence, you can break bad habits and turn them into good habits, even if you get hit along the way. You may not win every battle. But as long as you keep fighting, you will become a champion.

Chapter 10: Keeping Score

Tracking your progress and reviewing and improving your game plan as your program progresses is critical to ensuring you achieve the results you want, stay motivated, and stay on track.

You drafted your game plan from a safe distance before you got into the heat of the action. Something unexpected may have happened. Feel free to change it. The Gameplan is a guide, not a rulebook. You can adjust and change as much as you like, as long as you get where you want to go within the timeframe you plan to use.

Make sure your program gets you closer to your goals and doesn't let you fall back into the bad habits you're trying to break.

A Record of Your Success
Track your performance against your game plan. I call this the "winning protocol". This will help you measure and see your progress as you advance through the program. It also helps you put together your next game plan when

you're ready to quit another bad habit. Record your performance against your goals in your Win Record. Identify defects. Be honest and fearless. Your victory log is yours alone.

Ultimately, when you reach your goals, your habit journal and winning record will help you identify the key factors that contributed to your success. By applying these key elements to other areas of your life, you can continuously make positive improvements and move closer to realizing your vision statement.

Weekly Progress Reviews

Set a period each week to reflect upon your successes. Create a new good habit by doing it on the same day at the same time each week so it's easier to remember. Ultimately, the closer you get to your goals, the more likely you are to get good news, so start looking forward to this time.

Weekly progress reviews should be as neutral as possible. Keep your emotions in check, set a winning record, and explain exactly what you did well and what you didn't. Setbacks and failures should be accompanied by an action plan to correct areas needing improvement. These can be inserted into the next week's schedule.

Celebrating Victories

Small rewards built into your game plan are important motivators, so don't skip them. Even if they are just trinkets or tokens of value, they have a very personal meaning because you had to acquire them.

For example, when someone struggling with alcoholism begins their 12-step program, they are given chips that celebrate the different stages of sobriety. These cheap plastic chips come in 30 days, 6 months, 1 year, and 10 years of sobriety periods. These chips have no real monetary value but are one of the most prized possessions to those who acquire them. Celebrate when your game plan is complete and your overall goals are met. Invite your loved ones to a celebratory dinner or throw a party. Not only do you deserve it, but celebrating your achievements reinforces your positive behavior and makes it easier to repeat the process as you deal with other bad habits you want to correct.

Taking It to the Next Level

You have completed your first game plan. You gave up bad habits and replaced them with good habits. What now?

You haven't achieved your vision statement yet. Based on your experience and success with your first game plan, apply these lessons to your next bad habit.

Where does it stop? When your vision statement is no longer the goal you want to achieve but describes your day-to-day life, you know you've reached your ultimate goal.

Breaking the Habit Permanently
This may be the end of this handbook, but it's not the end of the road for you. You still have a lot of bad habits that you need to correct before you can live the life you always envisioned. But now that you know how to do it, the experience of breaking your first bad habit will give you the confidence you need to continue your journey.

As I said at the beginning, you have the power to do whatever you set your mind to achieve. Now you know the truth of those words. Continue believing in yourself and never give up. You can change your world. Only practice changing one habit at a time. I wish you good luck!

Printed in Great Britain
by Amazon